Withdrawn

THE FIRST VIETNAM CRISIS

CHINESE COMMUNIST STRATEGY AND
UNITED STATES INVOLVEMENT,

1953–1954

STUDIES OF THE EAST ASIAN INSTITUTE

COLUMBIA UNIVERSITY

China and Vietnam are neighbors closely related like lips and teeth; our two peoples are brothers sharing the common weal and woe. We are both socialist countries; our solidarity is cemented and developed under the great banner of Marxism–Leninism, and is therefore indestructible. The people of our two countries have sympathized with and supported each other, and formed a military friendship ever since our struggles for national liberation and against imperialism.

CHOU EN-LAI, in a speech
delivered at a mass rally in
Hanoi, May 13, 1960

Local defense will always be important. But there is no local defense which alone will contain the mighty land power of the Communist world. Local defenses must be reinforced by the further deterrent of massive retaliatory power. . . . The way to deter aggression is for the free community to be willing and able to respond vigorously at places and with means of its own choosing. . . . We do not, of course, claim to have found some magic formula that insures against all forms of Communist successes. It is normal that at some times and at some places there may be setbacks to the cause of freedom. What we do expect to insure is that any setbacks will have only temporary and local significance, because they will leave unimpaired those free world assets which in the long run will prevail.

JOHN FOSTER DULLES,
January 12, 1954

THE FIRST
VIETNAM CRISIS

CHINESE COMMUNIST

STRATEGY

AND UNITED STATES

INVOLVEMENT,

1953–1954

by Melvin Gurtov

1967
COLUMBIA UNIVERSITY PRESS
NEW YORK & LONDON

The East Asian Institute was established by Columbia University in 1949 to prepare graduate students for careers dealing with East Asia, and to aid research and publication on East Asia during the modern period. The research program of the East Asian Institute is conducted or directed by faculty members of the University, by other scholars invited to participate in the program of the Institute, and by candidates for the Certificate of the Institute or the degree of Doctor of Philosophy. Some of the products of the research program are published as Studies of the East Asian Institute. The faculty of the Institute, without necessarily agreeing with the conclusions reached in the Studies, hope with their publication to perform a national service by increasing American understanding of the peoples of East Asia, the development of their societies, and their current problems.

The faculty of the East Asian Institute are grateful to the Rockefeller Foundation and the Ford Foundation for the financial assistance which they have given to the program of research and publication.

TO MY PARENTS

FOREWORD

President Lyndon B. Johnson argues that it was not he who made the fateful decision that put the United States into Vietnam, but President Eisenhower. American support to Vietnam, he goes on to say, has been continued through the administrations of three Presidents. The implication of President Johnson's argument is that those Presidents who followed Eisenhower, of which Johnson himself is one, felt bound to honor his commitment. And the implication is also that subsequent policy decisions about Vietnam were a natural outcome of that original commitment, including the decisions that turned American support for the South Vietnamese in an internal Vietnamese struggle into direct American participation as the principal belligerent in a "major land war in Asia," an outcome against which General MacArthur had warned so solemnly.

This book is a careful, scholarly study of that period, the crisis in Vietnam of 1953–1954, based on documentary materials, including the papers of Secretary of State John Foster Dulles, and on interviews with many of the men directly involved. It will be invaluable for those who want to understand how and why the United States first became involved in Vietnam and the extent of the commitments made at that time.

There have been a number of books about the French war in Vietnam, which ended in 1954 with the Geneva Agreements that separated Laos and Cambodia from the old Indochina and divided Vietnam itself into the Communist North and the non-Communist South. But this is the first study focused directly on the role of the United States in those events and on the policy struggle in Washington. It describes and analyzes the strategic and political issues as the makers of United States policy saw them, and it details the struggle between those who advocated direct American military intervention and those who wanted to keep the American commitment severely limited.

Because it is focused on Washington, *The First Vietnam Crisis* is also valuable as a case study of the policy-making process. Major decisions in foreign policy are never simple. There are reasonable and responsible differences of opinion when men deal with such formidably difficult problems. But the stakes in the major decisions of foreign policy are high—war and peace and the survival of the nation—and it is not surprising that men bring conviction and even passion to the conference table. It would, in fact, be cause for alarm if such serious matters did not evoke strong feelings. There are also competing interests involved, the parochial interests of each of the different departments of the government and the military services. The advocates of air power, for example, saw in Vietnam an opportunity to prove their dream that air power offered a key to the entire range of military threats, including the ambiguously limited jungle war of Vietnam. In the Army and in Congress, on the other hand, there were men who were just as deeply convinced of the exact opposite, that bombing would be indecisive and result only in the need to commit American ground power to retrieve our lost prestige. All these ingredients for a deadly serious struggle in Washington, and several more besides, were present when the decision had to be made on what American policy would be during the 1953–1954 crisis in Vietnam. In describing the interaction of these forces, this book contributes not only to the understanding of how and why this particular policy decision was made, but to something of how and why all policy decisions are made.

The First Vietnam Crisis, finally, deals with strategic and political issues that continue to be in the forefront of the foreign policy problems we face today. What is the role of military power as an instrument of international politics, to give only one example, and at what level will the use of force destroy the political objectives we seek rather than achieve them? President Eisenhower decided against direct American military intervention in the Vietnam war and against any "escalation" of the struggle. Yet he came very close indeed. The arguments for such an intervention were appealing and the political pressures were powerful, stemming not only from Air Force interests in the Pentagon but from the State Department and elsewhere in the government. In these and similar struggles over political and military strategy described in this book, there are lessons for today's problems in international politics—and tomorrow's.

ROGER HILSMAN
Professor of Government
Columbia University

PREFACE

Today's dilemma is the outgrowth of yesterday's unresolved problem. The present guerrilla war in South Vietnam has brought about the second confrontation of the United States and Communist China over the tumultuous Indochina region since the end of the Korean War. In the fifteen years since both sides made Vietnam a matter of high national priority, positions have hardened, commitments have deepened, and the danger of a major war has increased. But the elements of the dilemma and the reasons for its existence have not basically changed. This book, which attempts to recount and analyze the crisis of 1953–1954 by focusing primarily on perceptions and policies in Washington and Peking, is written in the belief that the Indochina war cannot stand solely as an historical incident; it lives also as a reference for today.

Like France before it, the United States has been forced into a greater commitment than had originally been foreseen or desired. Even if Peking and Hanoi should refrain from massive, direct involvement, the prospects in South Vietnam are for continued long-term war of attrition, with costs that will dwarf those incurred by France and the United States between 1946 and 1954. It is here that the West's position is the more vulnerable one. General Vo Nguyen Giap, the present Defense Minister of North Vietnam and guerrilla warfare commander of the Vietnamese Communists (Vietminh) from

1946–1954, pointed up a fundamental dilemma for the West when he remarked that a democratic nation "does not possesss . . . the psychological and political means to fight . . ." when confronted with protracted war.* Vietnam is again the acid test of this viewpoint.

The American decision to accept the challenge phrased by Giap and remain in South Vietnam until the attainment of a satisfactory peace represents a radical departure from the approach adopted in 1954. The United States then was, and now remains, the paramount obstacle to the emergence of a wholly communist Indochina; but in 1954, the Government chose to accept a negotiated cease-fire rather than enter, and possibly widen, the war. The policy of indirect involvement through moral and material support was proven as ill-founded for Washington as it was successful for Peking.

From the American perspective, the first phase of the Vietnam war—closing, as does this study, with the Geneva Conference—raised complex, yet fundamental, questions for decision-makers in Washington. Throughout this book, the answers to these problems will be revealed and, in chapter 8, analyzed; but the questions themselves should be enumerated at the outset as follows:

1. Without doubt, the basic problem was whether and to what extent to become involved on the side of a colonial regime lacking popular support. Realizing full well that our French ally aimed pre-eminently at protecting its Far Eastern empire, were we to deny or lend it support in view of the implications for Western and American security of a Communist victory in Indochina? Were we to align against the forces of nationalism, even though communist-dominated, or were we to remain neutral and refuse assistance to an important ally?

2. If our highest interests required that the "colonialism"

---

* Quoted in Bernard B. Fall, *The Two Viet-Nams* (New York, 1963), p. 113.

issue be put off to the future, could we assure for ourselves a role in decision-making, military and political, over Indochinese affairs by virtue of our aid leverage? Or were we compelled to adopt a "French" policy and accept a position of minimal influence because we feared antagonizing an ally already under strong pressure at home to seek less than victory?

3. Did the handing over of a set policy toward Indochina from one administration to another preclude the revision of that policy? Could the inheritor alter his inheritance, or was he condemned to fulfill the letter of his bequest? When confronted with the knowledge that colonialism and the frustrated desire for independence were the chief obstacles to victory, had the time come for a reassessment of policy, or was change inconceivable precisely because a past policy existed?

4. When reports began filtering in of an enemy buildup in Vietnam, and of a constancy in enemy victories, was it time to inquire into the possibility of an intelligence deficiency in Vietnam? Since intelligence is one determinant of policy, was it proper to ask: From whom are we getting information? Who are we sending to the front for reports? Why are reports uniformly optimistic when the objective situation has shown a steady deterioration for years? Or, to the contrary, were there sound reasons for not asking these questions?

5. If the prevention of a Communist victory in Indochina and the maintenance of our alliance system were matters of equally high policy, were a regional defense organization for Asia and an early sounding of allied viewpoints immediate necessities?

6. Finally, did the fact that the French differed with us over the primary purpose of the war imply that they would also differ with us over conduct of the war, ways of achieving the peace, and particulars of a settlement?

From the Chinese side, the usual lack of information is no

more sorely felt than when attempting to recreate and trace the patterns of thinking that occur in the making of Peking's foreign policy. Although conjecture becomes a necessary evil, it does seem possible and desirable to outline certain of the questions that the leadership in Peking must have pondered in the period under consideration. These questions may be listed as follows:

1. With the death of Stalin, the great costs of war in Korea, and the armed presence of the United States in Asia, what policy could be constructed that would continue the Chinese commitment to Vietnam without risking general war, and yet would enable China to rebuild its economy?

2. As the United States increased its economic and military aid to the French, was it feasible to increase China's aid to the Vietminh?

3. What meaning did uncertainty over the composition of the new Soviet leadership have for China's foreign policy?

4. What did the decision to convene a Geneva Conference on Indochina indicate for China with respect to the Vietminh and to overall strategy in Asia?

5. Did the benefits of concluding a settlement in Indochina outweigh the costs of prolonged fighting?

The present study will focus on these key questions, for the answers to them formed the bases of policy in Washington and Peking. It will be seen that neither the United States nor Communist China could adopt a totally independent policy line, that both were strongly influenced by other powers and other considerations far removed from the Indochina scene. For both "outside" actors, policy toward Indochina involved striking a compromise; and to a large extent, recognition of the necessity for such a compromise determined the degree of success or failure of policy. Operating within different contexts, then, both the Americans and the Communist Chinese were confronted with similar problems in formulating a policy and influencing the conduct of an ally's war. The

Vietnam crisis is hence as much a case study in the ongoing complexities of policy-making as a reevaluation of an historical event with contemporary relevance.

MELVIN GURTOV

Santa Monica, California
October, 1966

ACKNOWLEDGMENTS

A book is the product of many minds but the responsibility of only one. Among those who have contributed toward making this work possible, I would like to express my gratitude to two scholars in particular: O. Edmund Clubb, whose careful attention to detail has promoted greater accuracy, and Roger Hilsman, whose insistence upon clarity has led to several revisions for the better. To them goes my hope that their assiduousness has been properly rewarded in the final product, although, of course, I accept full responsibility for all errors and deficiencies therein.

The First Vietnam Crisis is the outgrowth of research begun in 1962 and presented to meet in part the requirements for the Certificate of the East Asian Institute, Columbia University. I am pleased to thank the Institute, and especially its director, James W. Morley, for generous financial support during the summer of 1965 which made possible additional research and the putting of the manuscript into book form. Additionally, my appreciation for assistance with materials is acknowledged to Joseph Buttinger, who put his invaluable personal collection of works on Vietnam at my disposal; to William S. Dix, Librarian of Princeton University, for permission to use and quote from the John Foster Dulles Papers; and to those men (listed in the bibliography) who gave liberally of their time for interviews.

The process of publication alternated between New York and Taipei. Throughout this occasionally agonizing experience, Mervyn Adams of the Institute performed ably the many administrative functions vital to giving a book life. In New York, Dale Anderson and Dorothy Kiehl typed portions of the final draft, while in Taipei, Jacqueline Bezio carried well the burden of typing the final copy.

I must, finally, add a special thanks for my wife, Rochelle, who not only proofread the manuscript but also unselfishly permitted Vietnam to become a part of our first two years of marriage.

M. G.

CONTENTS

ABBREVIATIONS

IN TEXT

ANZUS   Security treaty between Australia, New Zealand, and the United States.
CCP   Chinese Communist Party.
CPR   Chinese People's Republic.
CPSU   Communist Party of the Soviet Union.
DRV   Democratic Republic of Vietnam, or North Vietnam.
EDC   European Defense Community.
ICP   Indochinese Communist Party.
MAAG   Military Advisory Assistance Group.
MSA   Mutual Security Act.
NCNA   New China News Agency.
NSC   National Security Council.
SEATO   Southeast Asia Treaty Organization.
STEM   Special Technical and Economic Mission.
VNA   Vietnamese National Army.
VPA   Vietnam People's Army.

IN FOOTNOTES

AFP. U.S. Department of State, *American Foreign Policy, 1950–1955: Basic Documents* (Washington, D.C., 1957).

CB. American Consulate General, Hong Kong, *Current Background.*

CDSP. The Current Digest of the Soviet Press.

Cong. Rec. U.S. Congressional Record.

DAFR. Peter V. Curl, ed., *Documents on American Foreign Relations* (New York, 1954, 1955).

DSB. U.S. Department of State, *The Department of State Bulletin*.

Dulles Papers. John Foster Dulles Papers. Princeton University Library, Princeton, N.J.

GB, *Papers*. Great Britain, Foreign Office, *Papers Relating to Foreign Affairs Laid before Parliament* (London, 1953, 1955).

House Special Study Mission Report 1953. U.S. House of Representatives, Committee on Foreign Affairs, *Report of the Special Mission to Pakistan, India, Thailand, and Indochina*, H. Rpt. No. 412, 83d Cong., 1st Sess., May 6, 1953.

House Special Study Mission Report 1954. U.S. House of Representatives, Committee on Foreign Affairs, *Special Study Mission to Southeast Asia and the Pacific*, 83d Cong., 2d Sess., January 29, 1954.

Mansfield Report 1953. U.S. Senate, Committee on Foreign Relations, *Indochina: Report of Senator Mike Mansfield on a Study Mission to the Associated States of Indochina*, 83d Cong., 1st Sess., October 27, 1953.

Mansfield Report 1954. U.S. Senate, Committee on Foreign Relations, *Report on Indochina: Report of Senator Mike Mansfield on a Study Mission to Vietnam, Cambodia, Laos*, 83d Cong., 2d Sess., October 12, 1954.

NCNA. New China News Agency, Weekly Bulletin.

SCMP. American Consulate General, Hong Kong, *Survey of China Mainland Press*.

Senate Foreign Policy Hearing 1954. U.S. Senate, Committee on Foreign Relations, *Hearing on Foreign Policy and Its Relation to Military Programs*, Vol. 11, 83d Cong., 2d Sess., March 19 and April 14, 1954.

Senate MSP Hearings 1954. U.S. Senate, Committee on Foreign Relations, *Hearing on the Mutual Defense Assistance Control Act of 1951*, Vol. 11, 83d Cong., 2d Sess., June 4–22, 1954.

1. THE SINO-VIETNAMESE RELATIONSHIP

As the war in Korea drew rapidly to a close, the eye of the next international storm shifted southward to Indochina, a region in which conflict had been raging unabated since the end of 1946. Serious American interest in the area had begun only with the start of the Korean War in response to the possibility of direct Chinese intervention in Vietnam simultaneous with the North Korean aggression. But Peking's interest, particularly in Vietnamese affairs,* ran deeper historically and substantively. By 1950 many of the same Vietnamese revolutionaries who had earlier been schooled in Chinese political thinking and military tactics were receiving moral and material support and battlefield training from Communist China, a change-over that brought with it the emergence of the Vietminh as a communist-dominated national revolutionary movement. A brief look at the substance of each of these Chinese contributions to the developing Vietminh revolution is necessary if we are to decipher the nature of the conflict, the actors in it, and the threat eventually posed to American as well as French interests.

* Although "Indochina" refers to Cambodia and Laos as well as to Vietnam, the facts that the First Indochina War (as Bernard B. Fall has aptly called the conflict which lasted from 1946 to 1954) was Vietminh-inspired and conducted and that the war was for the most part confined to Vietnam make clear the reasons for dealing exclusively with Vietnam in discussing China's impact on the course of the war.

DEVELOPMENT OF THE VIETMINH, 1945–1949

Long before the Vietnamese Communists became serious contenders for Indochinese states that had been under French suzerainty since 1883, nationalist Vietnamese political organizations and organizers were being shaped by events or ideas across the border.

From 1912 on, when the first Vietnamese revolutionary party was established immediately following the Chinese Revolution of 1911–1912, there was a noticeably parallel trend in the paths of development of political parties in the two nations.[1] More importantly, men destined to become leading figures in the Vietminh struggle against the French were receiving valuable experience in China. Ho Chi Minh worked as an interpreter for the Russian advisory group in China during the short-lived period of Kuomintang (KMT)-Chinese Communist Party (CCP) alliance.[2] In 1925, however, he found time to organize the Revolutionary Youth League (Thanh Nien), the first Vietnamese Communist party. In the same year Truong Chinh was in Canton,[3] perhaps as one of about two hundred Vietnamese youths brought to China under Ho's influence for intensive training in the Thanh Nien.[4] And Pham Van Dong, one of Ho's earliest followers and the present Prime Minister of the Democratic Republic of Vietnam (the DRV, or North Vietnam), was also in China. He had found a haven in Whampoa, the military academy established through KMT-CCP cooperation in which a "great many Vietnamese youth received political and military training and organized propaganda squadrons secretly to return to Vietnam to promote revolutionary work.[5]

The Second World War provided Ho's followers with an opportunity to put their experience in China to use. The Vietminh (Vietnam Doc Lap Dong Minh, or Revolutionary League for the Independence of Vietnam) had been formed in May 1941 in Kwangsi Province largely through Chinese Nationalist efforts. On March 28, 1944, Ho, through a series of shrewd maneuvers, was able to announce from within China the formation of a Provisional Republican Government of Vietnam under KMT control and with a Vietminh minority.[6] With Japan's defeat, the Vietminh moved to consolidate control in their own country. While Nationalist Chinese forces, given right-of-way into northern Vietnam under the Potsdam Agreements, looted and pillaged in the occupation process, the Vietminh proclaimed a National Liberation Committee on August 16, entered Hanoi on the nineteenth, and received the grand seal of the abdicating Emperor Bao Dai on the twenty-third. These efforts culminated in "the master stroke" of the party, for on VJ Day the Vietminh was the dominant native power in the country.[7] On that day (September 2, 1945) Ho Chi Minh, before a cheering throng in Hanoi, read a declaration of independence that announced the formation of a Democratic Republic of Vietnam.[8] The so-called "August Revolution" now had a government.

In late 1945, with the Chinese removed from the north and the British from the south of Vietnam in favor of the returning Free French, Ho Chi Minh decided temporarily to align with the French. Rejecting the urgings of the Truong Chinh faction to work with the Chinese, Ho "dissolved" the Indochinese Communist Party (the ICP, created in 1931 to succeed the Thanh Nien and designed to embrace Cambodia and Laos as well as Vietnam) on November 11, with French assistance ousted the pro-Chinese elements from his personal entourage in the summer of 1946, and sought to base the Vietminh appeal strictly on nationalistic grounds.[9] An historic distrust of the Chinese,[10] together with a realization that economic aid could only be obtained from Paris, combined to move Ho away from the Nationalists who had given him his start.

But hopes for a rapprochement with Paris proved untenable and, contrariwise, Truong Chinh's continued advocacy of a

"Revolution for national liberation" [11] seemed a reasonable alternative. Under two agreements signed March 6 and September 14, 1946, the French retained an armed presence throughout Vietnam as well as control of a nominally independent Vietnamese republic within the French Union and the Indochinese Federation. The Vietminh found this situation intolerable but could not budge the French through discussions. With the collapse of talks, the Vietminh therefore joined ranks behind a nationalist, anti-colonialist banner that was steadily gaining popular support; they proposed "to strive to achieve military aims in order to realize our political aims." [12]

What in actuality was the August Revolution on the eve of Franco-Vietnamese war? The leading figures in the Vietminh had been groomed in China; select groups of Vietnamese nationalists had been brought into southern China for revolutionary study; and the leftist political orientation of early Vietnamese parties had paralleled developments in China. Despite these closely related factors, many in the West classified the impending struggle simply as a vigorous attempt by Vietnamese nationals to drive out colonialism and assert their country's independence.

Vietminh behavior between 1945 and 1949 appeared on the surface to support the view that the revolution had little connection with communism. But behind the 1945 "coalition government," the "dissolution" of the ICP, and the appeal to nationalism were more esoteric designs which promised a slow evolution of the Vietminh into a party openly committed by organization and ideology to the communist sphere. Although having come to power on the wings of strong anti-French sentiment, the Vietminh once in power adopted much the same general line already applied with success in China: utilization of revolutionary and nationalistic impulses as the springboard for the introduction of communism.

Accordingly, the drive to achieve national unity masked a typically Stalinist projection of the future: a "bourgeois-democratic revolution," anti-imperialistic in content, followed by a communist (socialist) revolution and the dictatorship of the proletariat.[13] In the first stage, primary reliance would be theoretically placed on the working class, not on the peasantry; non-communist nationalists were welcomed into a Lien Viet Front (Hoi Lien-Hiep Quoc-Dan Viet-Nam) that replaced the ICP. Between May 1946, when the Front appeared, and late 1949, when the ICP came back to life, political leanings seemed to take second place behind a genuine coalition. But those "independents" who had joined the Vietminh in 1945 because they "thought it was impossible for anybody to sacrifice the supreme national interests for the sake of just party power" were soon disenchanted.[14] By the summer of 1946 "the Viet Minh's energies were bent to one end: to eliminate, discredit, and terrorize its possible rivals." [15] The ICP, far from disbanded, continued to exist in fact as the Association for Marxist Studies under Truong Chinh, a pattern first set by the Soviet Comintern in 1943.

The war that broke out December 19, 1946, then, had motivations more profound than anti-colonialism. Through a series of tactical shifts, the Vietminh had managed to maintain the image of purely nationalist ambitions while maneuvering for sole domination of the country. The French, on their part, rejected the only terms on which a showdown battle could have been avoided—unequivocal recognition of Vietnam's complete independence—and determined not to yield a potentially rich dominion which, Paris concluded, would be no match for French armipotence. It was a war between a decidedly, though not yet openly, communist movement and a European power resolved to maintain its Asian outpost.

In late 1946 the Vietminh were unprepared for long-term resistance. General Giap had told a mammoth rally in Hanoi the previous March that war would be disastrous without aid from outside. He urged postponement of the revolution since, as the case of Soviet Russia had shown, "many people have been able to overcome difficulties in bad situations by knowing when to wait for an occasion more favorable to their progress." [16] With the victory of Mao on the China mainland in 1949, that "more favorable" moment arrived after a wait of nearly three years. Unknown to the French, who harbored hopes of quick victory, a communist China marked the turning point of the Vietnam struggle.

THE CHINESE COMMUNIST COMMITMENT, 1949–1953

The foreign policy adopted by the Chinese People's Republic (CPR) immediately following its conquest of the mainland went under the slogan of "leaning to one side," that of the Soviet Union. That policy connoted China's alliance with communist nations and parties throughout the world in an "international united front." Broadly speaking, successful revolutions required that national (communist) parties join hands with the international communist movement centered in Moscow. With words of advice that were just then being followed in Vietnam, Peking's official New China News Agency (NCNA) proclaimed on February 20, 1950:

. . . patriotism cannot be genuine patriotism unless it is integrated with proletarian internationalism. Their own experiences of struggle have convinced the Chinese people that only by leaning to one side, the side . . . headed by the Soviet Union, can any country either achieve or maintain genuine independence. This point is of special significance for the people of Southeast Asia. . . . [17]

But for a developing revolution such as the one in Vietnam, it was not enough merely to "lean to one side." Also imperative was the adaptation of China's revolutionary model to the objective situation in each insurrectionary state, exemplified by the CCP's successful adaptation of Marxist-Leninism to China's objective situation. From 1949 until late 1951, Chinese statements stressed that in "imperialist countries" the Russian Revolution was the model, but in "colonial and semi-colonial countries" the Chinese Communist revolutionary movement was the model.[18] And as the *People's Daily* made clear on June 16, 1950, Vietnam and Malaya were the primary loci to which the Chinese model applied.[19]

Successful insurrection in Asia required not only a pro-Soviet orientation and the Maoist blueprint of revolt, but actual assistance from the "international united front." Mao held in 1949 that "it is impossible for a genuine people's revolution to win victory in any country without various forms of help from the international revolutionary forces, and even if victory were won, it could not be consolidated." [20] And since Indochina was a national as well as a revolutionary interest,* the CPR evidently found considerable justification for taking an active part in French-Vietnamese hostilities.

The Chinese hence were immediately sympathetic to the Vietminh cause. In an address to a mass rally in Peking at the time of the Trade Union Conference of Asian and Australasian Countries on November 3, 1949, Liu Shao-ch'i stated that the Chinese working class, besides having to lead

* A "national" interest may be defined as a high-priority goal of Peking's foreign policy which arises out of an area's significant historical or geographical relationship to mainland China and for the achievement of which Communist China is relatively likely to take high risks. A "revolutionary" interest is a goal of relatively lesser priority under which Peking seeks to promote its interests, power, or influence in other areas through support of indigenous rebel movements, thereby taking less risks itself.

China's assistance to the Vietminh actually spanned both categories. In promoting the Vietminh effort, Peking's revolutionary interest was clear. Moreover, the much-publicized *People's Daily* and *Red Flag* editorials of March 8, 1963, commenting on "imperialist aggressions against China," which raised anew the question of "unequal treaties" in light of the Sino-Soviet dispute, also made prominent a 1954 history manual published in Peking that claimed as "Chinese land prior to imperialistic encroachments" all of Indochina. French acquisition of Indochina in 1883 was therefore "illegal" from the start; the peninsula was always Chinese territory, and hence a national interest of the CPR. See Jacques Jacquet-Francillon, "The Borders of China: Mao's Bold Challenge to Khrushchev," *The New Republic*, April 20, 1963, pp. 18–22.

in the internal economic struggle, also would need "to shoulder the grave responsibility of assisting the working class and working people of capitalist countries and especially of colonial and semi-colonial countries in Asia and Australia. The victorious Chinese working class cannot and must not evade this honourable international responsibility. . . ." [21] Liu was more precise three weeks later. His oft-quoted speech in the capital on November 23 to the same conference offers the best evidence of China's immediate concern for and interest in applying its revolutionary model to the neighboring countries to the south. Liu stated, quite inaccurately: "The war of national liberation in Viet Nam has liberated 90 per cent of her territory." Then, pointing to Vietnam and a host of other Southeast Asian areas as well, Liu continued:

The national liberation movement and the people's democratic movement in the colonies and semi-colonies will never stop short of complete victory. Their struggles are entirely righteous. . . . The great victory of the Chinese people has set them the best example. . . . [22]

Events in northern Vietnam dovetailed with Chinese concern over the fate of Ho Chi Minh's forces. In July 1949 it has been claimed that a pro-Chinese wing of the Vietminh under Truong Chinh put down a "Western" (pro-Russian) wing. [23] The desire for aid from China probably also weighed heavily in Ho's congratulatory message to Mao Tse-tung on December 5, 1949. In it the DRV leader allowed himself to forget momentarily the traditional hostility of the two peoples when he wrote:

Brotherly relations have existed between the Vietnamese and Chinese nations during thousands of years of history. Henceforth these relations will be even closer for the developments of the freedom and happiness of our two nations, as well as for the safeguard of world democracy and lasting peace. [24]

The basic confluence of Chinese Communist and Vietminh ambitions in Indochina paved the way for initiatives at various political levels. On January 14, 1950 Ho Chi Minh proclaimed the readiness of the DRV to establish diplomatic relations with all nations under the claim that his was the only legitimate government of Vietnam. One day later the foreign minister of the rebel government, Hoang Minh Giam, notified Foreign Minister and Premier Chou En-lai that the DRV formally recognized the People's Republic and wished to exchange ambassadors.[25] On the eighteenth of January the CPR answered favorably; the Soviet Union did not follow suit until January 31. At another level, important fronts for political exchanges were set up on February 6, 1950 through a Sino-Vietnam Friendship Association. Again, the Soviet Union followed the CPR; a Soviet-Vietnam Friendship Association was not formed until June.[26] At least one purpose of the Sino-Vietnam association was to urge better relations between Vietnamese and overseas Chinese. A Vietminh broadcast related that the association was formed through the joint cooperation of "Vietnamese people's communities and the Chinese resident organizations. . . ." It advised that comrades "eliminate the old concepts regarding the Chinese residents" in southern Vietnam, where the bulk of the overseas communities existed, and "form a true friendship, which constitutes valuable cement for building a Sino-Vietnamese democratic bloc capable of annihilating any imperialistic gang." [27]

A final instance of political coordination arose when Hoang Van Hoan presented his credentials to Vice-Chairman Chu Teh on April 28, 1951 and took up residence at Peking as the DRV's "representative" or "delegate." The appointment came fourteen months after the mutual exchange of diplomatic recognition, and not until October 10, 1952 did the New China News Agency announce officially that Hoang had indeed taken up his post.[28] The Chinese, on the other hand, did not dispatch an envoy until September 1954 (when the Geneva Agreements had been signed and sealed); it was only then that Hoang was elevated to the rank of full ambassador.[29] The

Chinese clearly intended that high-level diplomatic dealings be kept under wraps.

Chinese recognition and the establishment of official political relations were the forerunners of more concrete signs, first, that Marxist-Leninism was a deep-rooted element in the Vietminh and, second, that Peking intended to back expressions of concern over the fate of the Vietminh revolution with deeds. As to the first, no doubts could remain by late 1949 that Ho Chi Minh had—as a broadcast vaunted—taken "over the ideas of President Mao Tse-tung to adapt them to the situation in Vietnam." [30] It has been maintained that Ho visited Peking in February 1950, and that one purpose was to receive instructions on the course of the August Revolution. According to Hoang Van Chi, Ho "had been criticized by Chinese theoreticians for being 'rightist.' They had argued that Ho was devoting too much attention to the patriotic war with the French and not enough to the establishment of communism." [31] Whether under Chinese pressure or not, the subsequent change-over by the Vietminh from a strictly anti-imperialist appeal to a public embracement of communist doctrine was directly in accord with Chinese Communist revolutionary dogma. The Dang Lao Dong (Vietnam Labor Party), a reincarnation of the ICP formed in February 1951, issued a Manifesto following its party congress that same month which clearly reflected the primacy of Chinese Communist ideology.[32] And in the shift from "anti-imperialism" to "anti-feudalism," the Manifesto provided a sure indicator of adhesion to the traditional Stalinist pattern of struggle in Asia. While stating that anti-imperialism was "the main task in the present stage," the document for the first time revealed that the ultimate goal of the August Revolution was the elimination of feudalism and the passage to socialism.[33] In short, the future course of communism in Vietnam would be guided by a blending of the very best Stalinism and Maoism had to offer.

Chinese insistence upon placing the party in the vanguard, a principle likewise spelled out in the Manifesto, together with Ho's personal acquaintance with the sudden terror that marked the end of the CCP-KMT alliance in 1927, soon made a mockery of the document's call for continuation of the united front. As 1951 closed, the Lien Viet crumbled altogether before a strongly centralized Lao Dong whose secretary general was Truong Chinh. The nationalists, whose support was previously vital to the maintenance of a convincing facade, were swiftly purged.[34] In much the same way as the CCP, the Lao Dong turned out those who, by having joined, permitted the party its first breath of life. Two years after the Chinese victory across the border, the Vietminh possessed the essential vehicles for Communist success in struggle: the Party, a nominally united front, and, as we are about to discuss, an army on the verge of new victories.

The dramatic changes in Vietminh political tactics were reinforced by help from Communist China. Until the Communist victory on the mainland, the military engagements in Indochina constituted not full-fledged war but a series of local engagements confined to northern Vietnam. But by 1953, when Chinese aid reached meaningful proportions, full-scale conflict had come to Indochina; Vietminh forces were no longer roving bands of insurrectionaries living on a prayer, but well-organized, Chinese-equipped and in some instances Chinese-advised units prepared for major thrusts not only in their own country but in Laos as well.

Prior to the establishment of Communist control on the Vietnam frontier, the forces that collectively bore the name "Vietnam People's Army" (VPA, officially founded December 19, 1944) derived their weapons from three sources: French soldiers killed in action, Nationalist Chinese willing to sell weapons for gold,[35] and Japanese weapons of World War II vintage. In addition, the Vietminh then and throughout the war manufactured weapons themselves at makeshift arsenals in fixed base areas.[36] But until the Chinese decided that material assistance was vital to Vietminh victory, the weapons at the rebels' disposal were meagre in comparison with those in French hands. Obviously, then, the triumph of the CCP generated not only a political shakeup but also a surge of anticipation of aid in the Vietnamese Communist camp. Vietminh expectations were quickly met. By late 1949 Chinese troops were already massed on the Vietnamese border, prepared to equip and train Ho's VPA "with full impunity."[37] Even before the better known use of Manchuria in the region north of the Yalu River as a sanctuary beyond which United Nations forces in Korea were denied entrance, the Chinese had utilized the three border provinces of Yünnan, Kwangtung, and Kwangsi as bases for the supplying and training of Vietminh forces. In effect, Mao's original formulation on the need for guerrilla base areas had simply been extended. In pursuit of injecting Communism into Vietnam and then using the Vietminh regime as a wedge into surrounding, non-communist territory, a good portion of southern China contiguous to northern Vietnam became an active sanctuary without the CPR's assumption of the role of a combatant.

The full measure of Chinese concern for Vietnam became apparent following Ho's trip to Peking. Mao is said to have answered Ho's request for assistance with the dispatch of General Lo Kuei-po (later the first ambassador to Hanoi) to serve as military advisor to the VPA.[38] Chinese administrative experts were sent along as well; to China came Vietminh officers to receive training and, according to a Communist source,[39] a delegation of male and female Vietnamese youths "to study revolutionary experiences and various kinds of techniques of construction." Soon afterwards actual Chinese arms deliveries began. Before the end of February 1950, French military circles began to notice heavier arms and a higher morale in the VPA, perceptible in the switch—albeit short-lived—to conventional attack.[40] First reports of "regular contact" between the CPR and retreating Vietminh troops appeared a short time thereafter, along with dubious French assertions that some Chinese "junior commanders" were leading Vietminh units in localized border skirmishes.[41] In the same period, Communist Chinese border forces were directly accountable for the appearance of Vietminh units bearing "heavy mortars and pack howitzers, followed shortly thereafter by complete artillery battalions using American-made recoilless rifles and 105mm howitzers."[42]

The fear attributed to a "high French personage" that Chinese aid could weigh heavily in the war if aid became "a matter of high Peiping policy"[43] soon materialized. While Chinese contributions did not enlarge Ho's arsenal to the extent that it equaled French weaponry, they nevertheless radically altered the military situation. For the first time outfitted with modern weapons, the Vietminh inflicted some severe losses upon the French in the north. These VPA successes were part of General Giap's "Operation Le Hong Phong I," in which the aim was to capture control of the border region and provide for easy passage of arms between Red China and the DRV. On October 12, 1950 the Communists' official Vietnam News Agency reported "complete victory" in the northern sectors comprising the Cao Bang-Dong Khe-That Ke triangle.[44] Giap's operation had thus been successfully completed, and with that "almost the whole northern half of North Viet-Nam had become a Viet-Minh redoubt. . . ." Of equal importance, the enormous quantities of French weapons lost to the rebels provided a constant source of arms not only for the regular fighting machine but also for new recruits from among the peasantry.[45] By the end of 1950, as one French observer noted, "The conditions of combat were profoundly modified to our disadvantage. Through the ever widening breach of the open frontier, Chinese aid was going to make the Vietminh an adversary more and more difficult to defeat."[46] As it was for MacArthur when the Chinese swarmed across the Yalu into Korea, so it was for the French here—a new war.

Once the Korean War ended, Chinese logistical know-how was transferred to the VPA [47] along with shipments of "light weapons, some trucks, and radios (all of American manufacture and captured from the Chinese Nationalists some years before). . . ."[48] French sources reported that, despite the Korean truce, total monthly tonnage sifting across the China border did not increase markedly in mid-1953 over the previous average;[49] but the French commanding general for the North Indochina district observed that for the first time deliveries had been made of 105mm field guns and bulldozers for road repairs.[50] Later Congressional testimony disclosed that the sources of these and other heavier manufactured items were not only Communist China but also Soviet Russia and the Skoda munitions works in Czechoslovakia.[51]

The fact was, however, that Red China, especially in its nascent condition, was hardly a bottomless reservoir from which economic assistance and military aid could be indiscriminately bestowed. Almost certainly as a consequence of economic needs at home and the tremendous burdens imposed upon industry and finances by the Korean conflict, Chinese aid to the DRV did increase over the years,[52] but its precise nature, amount, and moment of dispensation depended chiefly upon the shifting tides of fortune in the war. "China," Robert Guillain has explained, "adheres to a very simple principle: that the balance of power never inclines in any permanent manner toward the French side. There is no need—[and this is] the difference from what has happened in Korea—of direct intervention, of an invasion."[53] Thus, when France began using Vietnamese troops and receiving more American aid following the Korean War, the Chinese in turn stepped up their own aid program just enough to re-establish *l'équilibre*. When French fortunes rose, so did Chinese aid;

the Indochina campaign eventually became a crude game in which the French could never permanently regain the high ground.

While both Communist parties to the war maintained a strict silence concerning aid, with the Vietminh reluctant to glorify Peking's efforts and the Chinese mute on their contributions, the topic was of paramount importance by late 1953 not only to the Vietminh war effort but (as we shall see) to Paris and Washington as well. For by that period, although the Chinese were omitting aircraft from their arms deliveries (thus conceding the French total air superiority) and were content to have the Vietminh conduct their operations entirely on the ground, the trend of the war in the Communists' favor was undeniable. Autumn 1953, in fact, witnessed both a change and an increase in Chinese aid. From that point on, the Vietminh received trucks and light and heavy weapons, including bazookas, mortars, and cannons, sufficient to outfit and transport heavy artillery units for what proved to be the war-ending offensive.[54] Yet the way in which the aid was applied—the ability of the Vietminh faithfully to adapt the military and political elements of Maoist guerrilla strategy— determined the outcome of the August Revolution to no less an extent than arms shipments from Chinese arsenals.

The guerrilla warfare doctrines of Mao Tse-tung, set down in detail during the War of Resistance against Japan (1937–1945), provided the Vietminh's greatest source of potential danger to the continuation of French rule. Chinese Communist political and military experiences prior to the conquest had long been subjects of study by the Vietminh. By 1951, for example, between thirty and forty different books dealing with the Chinese Communist revolution had been translated into Vietnamese, primarily through Ho Chi Minh's initiative.[55] Both General Giap and Truong Chinh were ardent students of Chinese writings. Giap is said to have told a group of cadres, in the aftermath of the decisive victories on the Sino-

Vietnamese border late in 1950: "From this war, we will even more fully understand the greatness of Mao Tse-tung's thoughts. We hope that everyone will make increasing effort to study Mao Tse-tung's thoughts, and especially his military theories." [56] The general evidently capitalized on his own admonitions, for his conduct of the war against the French manifested an unspoken but inveterate allegiance to the military doctrines of Mao. Indeed, "the war the Vietminh fought in northern Indochina followed his [Mao's] teachings phase by phase despite the claims of Vietminh leaders that they improved on the doctrines." [57]

Although Giap formulated and restated Mao's views most extensively,[58] it was Truong Chinh who first adapted Chinese Communist strategy to the August Revolution while secretary general of the ICP. Having studied Mao's *On the Protracted War* and *On the New Stage*, Truong synthesized the general principles of the Chinese experience and Vietnam's struggle in his *The Resistance Will Win* (1947).[59] A detailed review of Truong's strategic exposition would be out of place here. Suffice it to say that, like Mao, Truong set forth a three-stage evolution of the war pattern—guerrilla warfare, mobile warfare, and positional or conventional warfare—which the Vietminh essentially adhered to throughout the war. The emphasis with Truong was on a popularly based and protracted war which would be decided not simply by the army's ability gradually to erode the enemy's strength but more importantly by success in acquiring peasant support. Just as Mao used the analogy of fish in the water to illustrate the importance of good army relations with the people, so did Truong when he concluded: "*The people are the water and our army the fish. The people constitute an inexhaustible source of strength to the army.*" [60] Mao's strategic insights were influential to the point of being plagiarized.

Despite assiduous efforts to cultivate peasant support in the northern areas through implementation of the "anti-feudalism" policy,[61] and despite renewed measures aimed at politicization of the VPA with Lao Dong cadres,[62] there is abundant evidence that neither line was smoothly achieved without commission of grave political mistakes and tactical blunders in the field.[63] Still in all, the unmistakable strengthening of the Vietminh by late 1953 demonstrated that the DRV hierarchy had been able to overcome major party and army deficiencies. What French successes on the battlefield there were between 1951 and 1953 were more the product of Vietminh audacity and overconfidence than of renewed French vitality. Only when the VPA departed from normal guerrilla tactics and deployed for set-piece battles in conventional formation were the French at an advantage. When the Vietminh stuck to a long-range strategy of attrition, they defied all the traditional methods of warfare known to French military leaders. For French commanders, the best weapon would probably have been a copy of Mao's writings, which clearly foretold the tactical sequence the VPA would need to follow to attain victory.

Instead, the French built their strategy around attack from reinforced concrete fortresses; some 1500 were constructed in 1951 alone.[64] From these fortified centers so-called pacification forces radiated outward for mop-up operations. Spacing its manpower throughout the north in this way, the French unwittingly cancelled out their overall numerical superiority; small guerrilla bands could effectively tie down larger enemy forces in individual battles. The result was a strategy disturbingly similar to Chiang Kai-shek's during the fruitless civil war against the Chinese Communists: a "fortress complex" in which consistent defeats produced a defensive psychosis, loss of initiative, and over-reliance on cities and blockhouses for protection. With the countryside thus exposed, Vietminh guerrillas fully exploited mobile warfare to win over the peasantry without the sacrifice of choice over the time and place of battle.[65]

The favorable trend of the war by late 1953 permitted the DRV new latitude both politically and militarily. On the diplomatic end, Ho Chi Minh, responding to a major peace initiative by French Premier Joseph Laniel on October 27, offered to negotiate an armistice. In reply to a questionnaire submitted by a correspondent for the Swedish newspaper *Expressen*, Ho cited one precondition: France had to recognize Vietnam's independence.[66] The reply was given November 20 and was published November 29, 1953. Between those dates, French forces under General Henri Navarre for the second time occupied the strategic garrison of Dienbienphu in northwest Vietnam on the twenty-sixth and ordered the further fortification of the fortress. For Paris, the retaking of Dienbienphu represented an important phase of the much publicized and highly optimistic Navarre Plan (discussed below). The plan, and the lack of specifics in Ho's offer, made the latter totally unacceptable.

Unruffled, the DRV twice more extended peace feelers. Sometime in December the DRV reportedly declared its readiness to negotiate if France "really respects the independence of Vietnam. . . ." Yet no concrete intentions could reasonably be attached to this second notice, for it was delivered in the most circuitous manner. Originating in the Vietminh information agency, it was picked up in Shanghai in a Tass dispatch and beamed to the West by Radio Moscow.[67] Within days, however, the offer was repeated. Ho Chi Minh took the occasion of the seventh anniversary of the Resistance War (December 19) to assert once more his government's desire for peace.[68] But the proposal still failed either to convey the place at which talks might be held or to propose their scope. And the timing seemed to indicate an attempt to capitalize on a change in power in Saigon. Premier Nguyen Van Tam had just then resigned from the Vietnamese government in favor of the more nationalistic Prince Buu Loc, Emperor Bao Dai's cousin and Vietnamese high commissioner in Paris.

As in 1946, the breakdown of a framework for negotiations opened the door to military action—here, to the decisive VPA counteroffensive, a vigorous campaign that would last from the winter of 1953 through the next summer. General Giap, who had probed with his army into Laos the previous April only to withdraw with the approach of the rainy season, launched a second invasion on December 24. The assault cut Laos in half with the seizure of Thakhek on the Laotian-Thai border (December 28). By January, Giap's forces menaced the more southerly frontier town of Savannakhet,[69] posing for France the prospect of an enlarged combat theatre.[70]

A rebellion which the French had hoped to quash in short order thus entered a new and dangerous stage by January 1954. The Vietminh leadership, guided by a common experience in Republican China, strongly influenced by Chinese Communist revolutionary tactics and political experience, and powered by an army trained, outfitted, and advised in the CPR, gave every indication that it could hold its own against superior arms and manpower. United States faith and prestige were therefore vested in a cause that had been steadily deteriorating since 1952 and that had evinced no capacity for reversing the tide. Loss of the Indochina peninsula to Communist forces was a very real possibility. Equally real to Washington officials, with the Panmunjom armistice signed on July 27, 1953, was the chance that the Chinese, as General Mark Clark warned, would turn south.[71] American policy-makers consequently determined that firmer steps be taken in Indochina. If overt Chinese intervention could be deterred, French recovery of the offensive was believed still possible. From 1953 until early spring 1954, American statements on the war in Indochina were weighted with measured words of caution directed at the Chinese and of alarm directed at Congress and our European allies. It is to these statements and their background that we turn now.

2. OUT ONE DOOR AND IN ANOTHER: THE AMERICAN COMMITMENT

By the time the Eisenhower Administration took office, the war in Indochina had already attracted the elements necessary for a major East-West crisis. Communist China and Soviet Russia were lined up behind the DRV, while the United States was already committed to support of the French. The new American government had inherited, rather than originated, the guidelines of policy toward an Asian battleground almost obscured by the Korean conflict. The basic question posed for the President was not whether to mold an Indochina policy, but how best to continue a policy begun under his predecessor.

BACKGROUND TO INVOLVEMENT

To understand the situation into which the Eisenhower Administration stepped in January 1953, a brief review of the Indochina scene from the perspective of American policy is necessary. Almost a year before Japan's capitulation, President Franklin D. Roosevelt had been aware that France, the Netherlands, and Great Britain would attempt to re-secure their prewar Far Eastern dominions. The President on several occasions held that these colonies should be placed under the United Nations trusteeship system as a first step toward eventual self-government.[1] Indochina was particularly on the

President's mind, for "France had done nothing to improve the natives since she had the colony." [2] French repossession of Indochina proved unpreventable, but until the extension of diplomatic recognition to the DRV by the Soviet Union and Communist China, United States policy retained Roosevelt's sentiments. Caught between the cross-currents of aid to an ally (the French) and sympathy toward a Vietnamese independence movement (led by the Vietminh), President Harry S. Truman chose not to provide Paris with the means of defeating the VPA and reimposing colonial rule. [3] American neutrality came to an end under the impact of events in and around Vietnam. Emperor Bao Dai had been in Europe since January 1948, refusing to return home until France offered meaningful political concessions that would give him de facto ruling powers. [4] As early as August 20, 1945, five days after the unofficial Japanese surrender, the Emperor had made an eloquent appeal to Paris in which he warned that France either grant Vietnam independence or face rising hostility and defections to the Vietminh side. [5] It was, however, the nearness of a Communist victory on the China mainland, not concern about Vietnamese aspirations, that compelled France to draw up accords on March 8, 1949 at least super-ficially consonant with the Emperor's demands. The Élysée Accords, named for the palace in which they were signed, were a Pyrrhic victory for the Vietnamese. While Cochin China (southern Vietnam) was permitted to become part of the Vietnamese state, Bao Dai agreed to commit his country as an Associated State within the French Union, with French control of foreign and military affairs. France, in substance, had retained control of its colony and gained the return of a prestigious Vietnamese hopefully capable of rivaling Ho Chi Minh for popular support. The Emperor, on the other hand, had "accepted terms which had been rejected by the Viet-namese delegation at Fontainebleau when they were put for-ward by the French Government in 1946." [6]

Awareness of what a Communist Chinese presence on the Vietnam border would mean for the VPA also caused France to look toward the United States for economic and military assistance. From the American standpoint, the French Expeditionary Corps represented the only present and effective counterweight to Communist armed power in Southeast Asia. Nevertheless, Washington desired that France first ratify the Élysée Agreements, thereby acknowledging the independence of the Associated States, before recognition could be granted and aid could begin to flow.[7]

The speed of the American reaction to French hopes for aid was augmented by Soviet recognition of the Ho government on January 30. In a press statement on February 1, Secretary of State Dean Acheson said Moscow's action "should remove any illusions as to the 'nationalist' nature of Ho Chi Minh's aims . . ."; he charged that it was "timed in an effort to cloud the transfer of sovereignty by France to the legal Governments of Laos, Cambodia, and Viet Nam . . ."[8] Taking its cue, the French National Assembly ratified the Élysée Agreements the next day. On February 7, Washington announced the extension of diplomatic recognition to each of the Associated States "as independent states within the French Union . . ."[9] The way was cleared for the first aid shipments in what was to become a large-scale American commitment.

The establishment of a communist government in China had pushed France into requesting, and obtaining, United States aid. Now, with the North Korean crossing of the 38th parallel, the Truman Administration sought further to bolster what Washington regarded as a vital anti-communist bastion in Southeast Asia. President Truman's June 27, 1950 statement indicating the dispatch of the Seventh Fleet to the Taiwan Strait publicly promised aid to the Indochinese states. In August, Robert A. Blum headed the first Special Technical and Economic Mission (STEM) of the Economic Cooperation Administration to Saigon. Subsequently, a Military Advisory

Assistance Group (MAAG) was also dispatched to administer separate military assistance, as well as to observe and report on the military situation through Army, Navy, and Air Force attachés. From the beginning the United States had been cognizant of the actual political stature assumed by the Associated States under the Élysée Agreements. Secretary Acheson's announcement of United States recognition had, in fact, specified that "this recognition is consistent with our fundamental policy of giving support to the peaceful and democratic evolution of dependent peoples toward self-government and independence."[10] President Truman, addressing Vietnam in the first Voice of America broadcast beamed to that country, likewise did not conceal American awareness that the Indochinese nations were not yet truly free.[11] In line with these viewpoints, Washington on at least two occasions in early 1950 sought, but failed, to persuade France that Bao Dai deserved more authority as a step toward real Vietnamese sovereignty.[12] These early episodes were edifying for the French: They showed that, by relying upon American support, French policy-makers in Saigon would be open to a certain measure of pressure from Washington. As the Vietminh had already learned, the acceptance of aid carried with it acceptance of "advice" from the granter. In 1950 American advice was limited; but as the war progressed and aid figures enlarged, the political impact of the United States' assistance program assumed increasing force.

Rebuffed in its attempt to wheedle concessions from France for the Vietnamese, the United States determined that France should at least not get credit for American economic assistance.[13] Much to the chagrin of French authorities, the economic and technical aid program was decided through cooperation agreements negotiated directly between the United States and each of the Associated States in September 1951. Largely through the efforts of Blum's economic mission, assistance was channeled directly to the Vietnamese, eliminating French middlemen and provoking French ire.[14] Aid in the nonmilitary category ran into high figures. Between 1951 and 1954 total economic and technical assistance was $96,-000,000, exclusive of a special $385,000,000 economic and military grant in September 1953 to spur the war effort[15] and of $800,000,000 earmarked under the Mutual Security Act for 1954.[16]

It was left to the French to administer the still greater amount under military aid, detailed in agreements signed during December 1950. Like Chinese aid to the Vietminh, the American program here climbed steadily, but at a higher level in tonnage, firepower, and dollar value. Military aid initially ranged from small arms to aircraft and naval vessels; it reached a peak during 1953 and 1954. By March 1953 the program included B-26 bombers, C-119 Flying Boxcars, tanks, and increased arms, ammunition, trucks, and medical supplies.[17] Technicians and pilot trainers were cast into the picture later. An estimate in mid-1954 placed the total value of American military supplies sent to Indochina since 1946 at over $2 billion.[18]

The Eisenhower Administration had, in summary, been left with little choice but to carry on the support program instituted under Truman. Committed to a costly ground war in Korea, Eisenhower recognized clearly the disastrous consequences if Truman's course were to be reversed: dooming the French to slow defeat, losing another area to Communist forces, emboldening the communist movement throughout Asia. The costs of keeping France in the war were bound to escalate, yet would be worth the price if Communist expansion could be prevented without sacrificing American lives. Percentage figures revealed Eisenhower's direction. Regularly scheduled American payments (both economic and military) accounted for 40% of the total war cost between 1951 and 1954; but the proportion reached 60% after the additional

$385,000,000 grant, and 78% by mid-1954. Surveying the Far Eastern situation in early 1953, the new Administration found itself in agreement with the Truman group on at least one count: The enemy wore a single face in Korea and Indochina, and had to be countered with substantial American help. As we shall now see, the combination of a general policy line inherited from Truman and a highly charged atmosphere that had existed in Asia since the end of World War II did much to propel Eisenhower toward a deeper involvement in Indochina than could have been foreseen.

FORMULATING AN INDOCHINA POLICY

The Eisenhower Administration's position was early expressed by the man who would ultimately play the leading role in attempting to save the region from the Vietminh. Writing in 1950, John Foster Dulles stated that

there is a civil war in which we have, for better or worse, involved our prestige. Since that is so, we must help the government we back. Its defeat, coming after the reverses suffered by the National Government of China, would have further serious repercussions on the whole situation in Asia and the Pacific. It would make even more people in the East feel that friendship with the United States is a liability rather than an asset.[19]

That the Government should go to great lengths to prevent a Communist triumph in Indochina was implied again by Dulles in a nationwide broadcast six days after taking office. Considering that "very great progress" had been made by the Soviet Union—China being subsumed under the Soviet bloc— in using "political warfare, and indirect aggression" to take over governments, Dulles turned to Indochina and commented:

If they [the Soviets] could get this peninsula of Indo-China, Siam, Burma, Malaya, they would have what is called the rice bowl of Asia. . . . And you can see that if the Soviet Union had control of the rice bowl of Asia that would be another weapon which would tend to expand their control into Japan and into India. . . .[20]

The Secretary of State's judgment of Indochina's importance received support a few months thereafter. A special study mission headed by Representative Walter Judd surveyed the Far East and also reported on the high stakes involved:

The area of Indochina is immensely wealthy in rice, rubber, coal, and iron ore. Its position makes it a strategic key to the rest of Southeast Asia. If Indochina should fall, Thailand and Burma would be in extreme danger, Malaya, Singapore, and even Indonesia would become more vulnerable to the Communist power drive. . . . Communism would then be in an exceptional position to complete its perversion of the political and social revolution that is spreading through Asia. . . . *The Communists must be prevented from achieving their objectives in Indochina.*[21]

The Judd Mission's conclusion was later taken up by President Eisenhower as the "domino theory": if Indochina fell, all Southeast Asia would be vulnerable to Communist infiltration and take-over. The warning of a chain reaction would help fix Indochina in the public mind, and the ominous notes contained in the speeches by Dulles and the Judd report would be sounded often by the Administration in ensuing months.

As the new Administration took over, the increasingly dangerous Indochina situation was complicated by sudden tension in nearby Thailand. On January 10 the Chinese Communist regime indicated that a Thai "autonomous government" would be set up in southern Yünnan Province, together with a joint autonomous government for the Thai and Shantou peoples in western Yünnan.[22] Although Premier Chou later asserted that the measure was in accord with the Communist policy of autonomy for all national minorities,[23] the measure may have been more than administrative or even defensive.[24] The about 200,000 Thais estimated to be in southern Yünnan (May 1953), when placed beside the "several hundreds of thousands" of Thais in northwest Vietnam,[25] posed the potential threat of a link-up and a movement diverted from nationalistic to pro-communist ends. Prince Souphanavong, leader of Pathet Lao forces which operated with Vietminh aid and direction, was considered a supporter of a "Greater Thai Federation." [26] And in Laos, Vietnamese constituted the third largest minority group. Moreover, Thailand itself had a substantial Chinese community of about three million; Chinese in fact formed the largest proportion of Thai communists.[27] These interrelated features of national groupings in Southeast Asia were cast into an already complex jigsaw puzzle and heightened the need for additional regional security measures.

Behind it, the Administration already had in hand, for defense of its Far East interests, a security treaty with Australia and New Zealand (ANZUS, signed September 1, 1951), and treaties of mutual defense with the Philippines (August 30, 1951) and Japan (September 8, 1951). All were in force by mid-1952.[28] But these, it was implied in Washington, were clearly insufficient to cope with the perilous Southeast Asia situation of the spring of 1953. In his State of the Union Message on February 2, Eisenhower promised "a new, positive foreign policy" from his Republican Administration, and as a beginning told of the removal of the Seventh Fleet from the Taiwan Strait separating Chiang Kai-shek's Formosa stronghold from the China mainland.[29] Secretary Dulles subsequently revealed that this move, which seemed aimed at unleashing Chiang's forces for the long-awaited attempt to recover the mainland, was being studied as part of a campaign to end the Indochina war by default of the Chinese. Under the Administration's new strategy, said Dulles,

Korea and Indo-China are two flanks. There is a large force [Communist China] in the center. If that force in the center can be without danger shifted to one flank or then the other flank it is very difficult to see how any satisfactory peace can be established either in Korea or in Indo-China. It is necessary, I believe, to create some sort of a threat in the center [the Nationalist Army] to hold and pin them down and then there is a better chance of getting some success of the two flanks. Now that program hasn't actually evolved yet into final form, there is a lot of work that has to be done. . . .[30]

Dulles explained further that ending the Indochina war would, in its turn, enable France to place her forces into the controversial European Defense Community (EDC) on a level commensurate with German contributions, thereby removing French fears of a German-dominated European army.*

The rationale behind this tentative, and apparently discarded, plan was the possibility, however remote, of a Chinese shift to the south after the conclusion of peace in Korea. To head off that contingency, the Government proceeded to elaborate the thesis that the war in Indochina was but an extension of the Korean battle line.[31] The United States and France reached an agreement on March 28 "that should the Chinese Communist regime take advantage of [the] armistice [in Korea] to pursue aggressive war elsewhere in the Far East, such action would have the most serious consequences for the efforts to bring about peace . . . and would conflict with the understanding on which any armistice in Korea would rest." [32]

President Eisenhower followed up the new line in the succeeding month. In a wide-ranging review of post-World War II American-Soviet relations before the American Society

* Remarks at the White House Conference for the Advertising Council, March 24, 1953, p. 9, in Dulles Papers [File I.B.1]. EDC, which was to figure prominently in the Indochina crisis, comprehended the integration of West German forces into a six-nation West European army. France, Italy, Belgium, the Netherlands, and Luxembourg were expected to contribute units, enabling the United States to decrease (but not eliminate) its European-based army. France, whose Premier René Pleven had first proposed the plan in September 1950, became the key to its approval. In January 1953 the EDC treaty came before the National Assembly for ratification, where it remained the subject of heated debate for the next year and a half. See Raymond Aron, "Historical Sketch of the Great Debate," in Daniel Lerner and Raymond Aron, eds., *France Defeats EDC* (New York, 1957).

of Newspaper Editors on April 16, 1953 he forged the link between the two war theaters more solidly when he declared: "For any armistice in Korea that merely released aggressive armies to attack elsewhere would be a fraud." The President called upon the Russians to cease their "direct and indirect attacks" in Indochina and Malaya, and to conclude an armistice in Korea. The free world, he cautioned the successors to Premier Josef Stalin (who had died on March 5), "knows that aggressions in Korea and in Southeast Asia are threats to the whole free community to be met only through united action." [33] Eisenhower had raised the possibility, not to have significance for several months, that active containment of the Communists was not restricted to Korea.

To the same audience two days later, Secretary Dulles was more specific. Administration policies gave "a new order of priority and urgency . . . to the Far East." The United States considered "that our Eastern friends, from Japan, Korea and Formosa, to Indochina and Malaya, face a single hostile front, to be met with a common purpose and growing co-operation as between the component parts of freedom." Directing attention to the new area of cooperative Western efforts against Communist expansion, Dulles asserted flatly that

the Communists in the Far East can no longer count on winning by shifting their strength and by focusing attack on one or another free world position that is isolated from the others. The Communist strategy, based on a contiguous land mass, is now confronted by a growing free world unity based upon the peninsular positions and offshore island chain now controlled by the free peoples of Asia.[34]

Whatever "growing cooperation" Dulles sensed did not diminish Vietminh audacity on the battlefield. Giap's first thrust into Laos on April 12, which carried to within thirty miles of the capital at Luang Prabang by the thirtieth, prompted a general mobilization by the Laotian government.[35] Washington responded quickly. From twenty-four to thirty-six troop-carrier planes of the C-119 type were made available to Laos to help blunt the invasion.[36] Dulles, appearing before a joint Senate-House committee hearing on the Mutual Security program, allowed that Indochina presented a serious threat and that the situation in Laos was "disturbing." If Indochina fell, he spoke of a "chain reaction" throughout the western Pacific.[37] But the spring offensive by the Vietminh in Laos, an intensified British campaign in Malaya against Communist rebels, and Peking's decision to establish a Thai Autonomous People's Republic also made aid to Thailand vital; that government, too, had declared a state of emergency. Upon appeal from Bangkok, therefore, Dulles announced on May 9 that "certain amounts" of small arms ammunition had been delivered, with "other military items" to follow.[38] The stain of crisis was beginning to deepen and spread.

But the true threat to Pacific security was still held to reside at Peking. To coalesce a unified lineup against future Chinese incursions, the foreign ministers of the United States, Great Britain, and France released a statement following a Big Three conference on July 14, 1953, in Washington, apparently designed to avoid the Acheson-MacArthur "perimeter line" miscalculations that preceded the North Korean aggression. "The Foreign Ministers were of the opinion," read the statement, "that an armistice in Korea must not result in jeopardizing the restoration or the safeguarding of peace in any other part of Asia. . . . They agreed that the struggle in defense of the independence of these three nations [the Associated States] against aggressive Communism is essential to the Free World. . . ."[39] Through the series of statements by Dulles, capped by the tri-nation agreement, the Administration had brought Indochina within the security "perimeter" of the United States and the Western world, apparently on the untested assumption—and a most significant one—that the interested states would *act* with what Dulles had termed "a common purpose and growing cooperation" if Indochina required further assistance.

The French were quick to grasp at these straws in the hope of some relief from the six and one-half year drain on their men and material. Foreign Minister Georges Bidault, on the day of the announcement of the armistice at Panmunjom (July 27), declared that the Korean War represented a signal triumph for collective security which he hoped would bring peace to Indochina as well.[40] Timed to coincide with an emphatic warning to Red China [41] against its resumption of aggression, issued by the sixteen members of the United Nations that had contributed to the Korean defense effort, Bidault's statement seemed to allude to another allied intervention, in Indochina, if circumstances so warranted.[42]

In ensuing months, strong words poured from the White House and from the State Department as well. Again the emphasis was on making American concern unmistakably clear by tying Indochina's defense to Southeast Asia's and invariably America's security. At the annual Governors' Conference in August, the "chain reaction" concept was invoked again when the President said that if Indochina fell by the wayside the Malay Peninsula "would be scarcely defensible," while other parts of Asia would be "outflanked" or "in no position for defense." If the situation thus evolved, Eisenhower asked rhetorically, "how would the free world hold the rich empire of Indonesia?" Under these circumstances, it was evident to him that "somewhere along the line, this must be blocked and it must be blocked now. . . ." He concluded by describing a successful Chinese Communist-backed movement in Vietnam as "something that would be of a most terrible significance to the United States. . . ." [43]

Secretary Dulles, having written of Indochina's importance to the free world's security years before, now joined in with a solemn warning to the CPR. Anticipating the "massive retaliation" doctrine (see chapter 4), he told the American

Legion Convention on September 2 that Korea's lesson was to "make clear our intention in advance" so that the aggressor nation would have to think twice before making an assault. Neither Korea nor the two world wars would likely have occurred had the enemy calculated the American response, a response that should have been made public "so that the potential aggressor will take this into his calculations." So doing, he predicted, "we shall probably not have to fight." [44]

Shifting from the more general to the specific, Dulles said that "A single Communist Chinese aggressive front extends from Korea on the north to Indo-China in the south. The armistice in Korea, even if it leads to a political settlement in Korea, does not end United States concern in the Western Pacific area." Having reiterated the Government's two-front Far Eastern policy, Dulles pointed out Chinese interference and warned in the most forceful manner to date against the CPR's involvement:

Communist China has been and now is training, equipping and supplying the Communist forces in Indo-China. There is the risk that, as in Korea, Red China might send its own army into Indo-China. The Communist Chinese regime should realize that such a second aggression could not occur without grave consequences which might not be confined to Indo-China. [45]

Dulles' statement had reached the uppermost limits of diplomatic language. The United States would not simply regard the subversion of Indochina as an act "of a most terrible significance" (Eisenhower's statement of the previous month). To avoid another enemy miscalculation, Dulles implied that the United States would take countermeasures against a Chinese attack that might well carry beyond the Vietnamese border onto the China mainland.

Here was the first concrete attempt by the new Administration to develop an alternative to what it considered the basically static and defense-oriented containment thesis. The Government would avoid involvement in another Korea-type fringe war by issuing an advance notice that it "might" strike at the source of the aggression. The potential aggressor, Communist China, would then freeze before the awesome power of the United States rather than face possible obliteration. In this thesis, the Korean situation had been reversed: Now it was the United States, not Red China, which drew the line and strongly intimated intervention as the consequence of a trespass. For just as Chinese intervention in Korea was in part attributable to a fear for their own security, so was American concern over Indochina linked to a potential threat to the United States. Three days after Secretary Dulles had put China on notice, Under Secretary of State W. Bedell Smith cautioned that the United States could not "be indifferent to this struggle" because Indochina's position had " a direct bearing on our own security." [46]

If the purpose of underscoring Indochina's security value and warning against direct Chinese intervention was merely to assure that Peking's role remained, like Washington's, that of supplier, the policy was an unqualified success.[47] The immediate and over-riding problem, however, remained unanswered. By the winter of 1953, with the Vietminh preparing for the decisive "general counter-offensive," the indications pointed inescapably to the fact that the chief threat to Indochina lay within, rather than outside, the region. The Administration, however, saw no immediate need to concoct a formula for dealing with the Vietminh. Instead, Washington concentrated on counterbalancing Chinese aid through increased economic and military assistance and moral support. Beyond those measures, little else would be ventured on the assumption that, over the long run, the balance of power would swing to the French. Chinese assistance was tacitly accepted; the Administration saw, but hesitated to act upon, the same set of circumstances that had confronted President Truman in Manchuria throughout the Korean conflict—an active sanctuary abetting a Communist military movement. Apparently, the only firm decision reached regarding the Chinese was that an armed attack from outside Indochina would be met directly by the United States.[48] In the absence of such an attack, Washington at this stage manifested full agreement with Senator Mansfield's assertion that "American aid . . . does not and should not involve the commitment of combat forces [to Indochina]. Sacrifices for the defense of freedom must be equitably shared and we have borne our full burden in blood in Korea." [49] These, then, were the American policy guidelines at the close of 1953; but the objective military situation argued strongly against their continuation, while the political picture showed similar cause for pessimism.

3. WASHINGTON AND PARIS: THE POLITICAL TANGLE

American endeavors to head off another "Korea" were complicated by fundamental political problems in Vietnam that exacerbated Franco-Vietnamese relations, severely hampered the war effort, and actually tied the hands of American policymakers. From the Vietnamese side, the demand was for a readjustment of their nation's position within the French Union to one of real independence. The French publicly countered that any change would have to await an end to the war; privately, they were averse to any political shakeup that might rock the boat of their whole colonial empire. The Americans, anxious to prosecute the war, adopted a stance designed to please both sides but which pleased neither.

Although Vietnam's status within the French Union supposedly comprehended all the attributes of a sovereign state, the power to exercise independence was basically absent. The various conventions signed by French and Indochinese representatives in 1949 and 1950 could not gloss over the hard fact that the Associated States were still colonies subject ultimately to control from Paris. The French Constitution, the governing instrument of French Union members as well as the Republic, did not provide a definition of "independence" applied to dependencies, nor did it use the words "independence" or "sovereign" in speaking of the Union.[1] To have altered the status of the Associated States would have required a consti-

tutional change; and France was chary of the wide repercussions that might erupt within its dwindling empire from out-
right recognition of any one colony's complete independence.
As one reporter noted, "A crack in the French Union any-
where would tend to weaken it everywhere." [2]
Some facts of Vietnamese life during the early fifties illustrate the subordinate position of the native government. The
Bao Dai regime shared with France control over public security, justice, and national defense. Vietnamese economic
independence was compromised by participation in a tri-
nation (Cambodia and Laos) customs union. And membership in the French Union cost Vietnam through the sharing
of "certain prerogatives." [3] Domestically,[4] dependency of the
piaster upon the French franc led to behind-the-scenes financial dealings to take advantage of higher exchange rates on
the piaster in Paris. News from Saigon was heavily censored
to bar criticism of the central government. French enterprises
enjoyed concessions on ownership rights and commodities produced, with labor and resource potential exploited for home
markets. Land reform, instituted in February 1951 and again
in June 1953, was carried out grudgingly and lackadaisically.
All the hallmarks of colonial rule—absentee landlords, conditions of serfdom, and the payment of usurious rates for rentals
or loans—could be found in the Vietnamese countryside. Prince
Buu Loc, who later became Premier and who was primarily
responsible for negotiation of the Élysée Agreements, commented in 1952 on the gaps in Saigon's sovereignty:

. . . national independence must be consolidated; the French Union
must be brought to a point of equilibrium so that it may offer
effective support to the sovereignty of its member states; and a
new Vietnam must be built with the help of a boldly reformist
nationalism.[5]

Until mid-1953, when Paris took the first tentative steps
toward satisfying Vietnamese demands, recurrent calls were

made warning that the French war effort was being distracted and diminished in the absence of a more practical political arrangement for the Associated States. A House study mission reported in May 1953:

Many Indochinese state that the unrest and failure to develop full support of the government is because they do not feel that they have had adequate assurance of their ultimate independence. . . .

It is believed that clearer and firmer commitment by the French on this question of independence will be effective in exposing fraudulent Communist promises, in uniting the forces of the Indochina area in their struggle against communism, and in the ultimate attainment of their independence.[6]

The mission's findings were substantiated the following month. On the basis of discussions with military and civilian personnel, aid officials, Frenchmen, and Vietnamese, Senators Everett M. Dirksen (Republican of Illinois) and Warren G. Magnuson (Democrat of Washington) reported back to the President with the suggestion that "a target [date] of independence" be established for Vietnam.[7]

From Saigon, Premier Nguyen Van Tam vented his nation's demand for a new treaty to replace the outdated 1949 conventions.[8] Particularly irksome was the question of French control over the armed forces. Although General Navarre claimed that extensive portions of Vietnamese territory were being turned over to the Vietnamese National Army (VNA),[9] the fact was that, by late 1953, only one Vietnamese had attained the rank of general in the French Army.[10] What this meant was that French officers monopolized the command posts in *both* the French Union and Vietnamese forces, a major factor behind the lack of initiative and enthusiasm among Vietnamese soldiers.[11]

By a declaration of July 3, 1953, France vowed "to complete the independence and sovereignty of the Associated States of Indochina."[12] As always, no date for independence was specified, and developments during the remainder of the year revealed that Paris was merely bandying about words. In November, Premier Tam was favorable to the French gesture, but was equally insistent upon full equality with France in an association of sovereign states.[13] In the intervening months since the July declaration, real self-government, with unfettered control over decision-making, had not yet come to Vietnam. As importantly, the non-Communist nationalists, whose support was vital to the attainment of widespread popular support, were not involved in government and defense duties.[14]

From the way the French were meting out piecemeal political "bonuses" during 1953, the unmistakable impression was that the military situation within each Associated State was determining France's political attitude, just as the victory of Chinese Communism had spurred ratification of the Élysée Agreements. With Laos, which had survived its first invasion in April, Paris concluded a "Treaty of Amity and Association" on October 8. The agreement recognized Laos as a "fully independent and sovereign State," in return for which Laos "freely reaffirms its membership in the French Union, an association of independent and sovereign peoples. . . ."[15] But efforts to slice through the intricate wording in discussions between President Vincent Auriol and King Sisavang Vong later in October failed to determine just how much independence the Laotians really had.[16] Only Cambodia, untouched by the war, was able to pressure the French for solid political concessions. Bilateral agreements arrived at between July and October 1953 at Pnompenh (the Cambodian capital) resulted in nearly complete autonomy by February 1954,[17] five months ahead of similar arrangements for Vietnam.

On the other side of the coin, the French argued, in certain respects convincingly, that real independence would eventually destroy all hopes of winning the war. For this reason, Paris would go no further than to grant (as in the Laotian case) complete independence *within* the French Union. Sharp debates in the French National Assembly in October cleared up the government's position. Premier Laniel stressed that if Vietnam were outside the French Union, France would have no obligation to protect her. To grant unencumbered sovereignty to a state which would then be unable to defend itself was ridiculous; independence within the Union was not only the sole policy acceptable to France, but also the only practical one.[18]

But behind the French contention that wartime prohibited further political steps was the more basic viewpoint that the Indochina situation was a domestic issue of interest only to Paris. Therefore, Indochina was not a proper subject of open debate in the United Nations and far less a subject for submission to the Organization as a threat to international security.[19] For one thing, France feared that action by the UN might precipitate Chinese intervention in the Korean manner, with the possibility of widening the conflict. Perhaps of greater importance, however, was that the compulsion to remain the de facto power over the Associated States, a legacy of the dying colonial era, persisted. President Eisenhower summarized French thinking:

At that time [1953] the French Government apparently saw no need to publicize any such sincere, simple, and selfless pronouncement. As far as I could tell, this reluctance seemed to have its source in the French conviction that making an all-out statement would weaken their leadership in the war and might have serious effects in other portions of the French Empire, including Algeria; moreover, the civil officials with whom I often talked . . . felt also that an announcement of voluntary withdrawal from the area during hostilities would be a tremendous blow to French prestige and influence in the world.[20]

Undercutting the French position was the deteriorating state of Bao Dai's restricted but functioning government. An alternative to Ho Chi Minh was the sine qua non of military success; without a government attuned to the needs of the populace, the invisible force of nationalism could never be harnessed to the side of a free Vietnam. But Bao Dai's government gave every sign of being unable to attract a large and influential body of support. Both before and after the French declaration of July 3, his government was the seat of widespread corruption, power struggles, and general ineptitude. Bao Dai spent most of his time at the official palace in Dalat or in Paris; he was rarely near his troops.[21] Unless an unqualified grant of independence could be coupled with solid political reforms within the native regime, the French would be fighting without a semblance of popular backing, vulnerable to Communist charges of "colonial imperialism."

Both the United States and Great Britain were openly critical of France's equivocal approach to the political problem, which was really at the core of the difficulties in Indochina. Prime Minister Churchill, addressing the Commons on May 11, 1953, censured France's refusal to take the war before the United Nations to remove the stigma of colonialism.[22] The American insistence upon French attention to the independence issue was obvious from the findings of a series of Congressional field studies during 1953, all of which held that French ambiguity was the chief impediment to successfully concluding the war. A House mission in May agreed with London in urging (among other things) that the war be placed before the Organization.[23] The House Committee on Foreign Affairs, reporting in June on the Mutual Security Act for 1953, enumerated in no uncertain terms the stakes involved in granting independence:

. . . large segments of the population, particularly in Vietnam, do not fully support the local government because they do not have the necessary confidence in its ultimate victory, nor in the ultimate willingness of the French to accord independence for the area. In their drive to take over Indo-China, the Viet Minh have appealed to the fervent nationalism of the people in attempting to retain a degree of control which is resented by the people who feel that they have not had adequate, firm, and unequivocal assurance of their ultimate independence. The testimony before the committee indicates that until the peoples of the Associated States are assured of receiving their ultimate independence, success in driving out the Communist invaders will be difficult, if not impossible, to achieve. . . .[24]

Nor, as already noted, did the July 3 declaration remove doubts of French intentions. A tour by Senator Mike Mansfield led to a warning that the "failure to utilize the indigenous power latent in nationalism merely serves to increase immeasurably the cost to ourselves and to France of preventing the Communists from seizing Indochina and it could even throw the entire issue into doubt." [25] Before the end of the year, two additional survey teams had come to much the same conclusion, and one went so far as to say: "The problem at this stage is more a psychological one than a material one." [26]

The President shared Congressional sentiment in this regard. He took the position that until the recognition of each State's complete autonomy, political support steadily accruing to the Vietminh side would continue. Pending a French policy revision, the President has written, "it was almost impossible to make the average Vietnamese peasant realize that the French, under whose rule his people had lived for some eighty years, were really fighting in the cause of freedom, while the Vietminh, people of their own ethnic origins, were fighting on the side of slavery. It was generally conceded that had an election been held, Ho Chi Minh would have been elected Premier." [27] Or, as a former Foreign Service officer commented tersely after his return to the United States following a five-year tour of duty: "The French-sponsored government of Bao Dai to them [the Vietnamese] is a mere continuation of the old colonial system under a new label." [28]

Washington's disturbance over French policy lay equally in our ally's reluctance to state that the war was more than a domestic concern, that it was primarily part of the Western front against the spread of communism. Eisenhower could therefore say that the refusal of France to lend an international, anti-communist flavor to the Indochina conflict "precluded the possibility that other free nations could help. . . ." [29] The United States, he reasoned, could not be party to a struggle that primarily was one to maintain a colonial empire rather than one to defeat communist aggression.[30]

It was becoming evident through the interchange of views among the three allies that any foundation for a united approach to the war was of quicksand quality. On both sides there were clear-cut inconsistencies of policy that held out the possibility of future misunderstandings. The French Government was certainly anxious to continue receiving American aid, without which its war machine would soon grind to a halt. But the French would not permit the intrusion of any power that might delimit or remove their absolute control of the war. The suspicion with which the American advisory mission was regarded, the ruling out of an appeal to the United Nations, and the various restrictions placed upon U.S. field personnel in Indochina [31] all brought into focus French concern about outside "intervention." General Navarre, upon his arrival to take over command of the Expeditionary Corps in May 1953, was disturbed to find the Americans sympathetic to Indochinese demands for complete independence.[32] His appreciation for American military aid did not dispel his conviction that the U.S. program was interfering with French policy-making; [33] subsequently, he would reject direct American training of Vietnamese contingents for the same reason. Nevertheless, while Paris was determined to avoid politically internationalizing the war, it was not averse to tying a final settlement in Korea to an end to the fighting in Indochina, thereby *extending* the area of allied concern. The French, in effect, wanted victory, but only on terms which neither infringed upon their specific interests in the region nor threatened to involve them in a larger war.

On the American side the perspective of the French prob-